The Perils Of Modern Society

(Rejection Of Capitalism and Observations Of Modern Society)

By: Joshua Douthett

Chapter 1: The Positives of Modern Society

It might seem unusual to open a book that critiques capitalism and modern society with an exploration of its virtues, but context matters. To understand why some systems and cultural norms warrant rejection or reform, we must first acknowledge what they have achieved. While the chapters ahead will dive deeply into the pitfalls and fractures of the contemporary world, this chapter is dedicated to celebrating the undeniable positives of living in the modern age. Compared to other eras of human history, today offers comforts, opportunities, and marvels once inconceivable. To dismiss these advancements outright would be to ignore the complexities and dualities of progress.

The Miracle of Technology

Technology, arguably the cornerstone of modern society, has transformed nearly every aspect of human existence. From the wheel to the smartphone, humanity's ability to innovate and iterate has culminated in a world where distances are bridged in seconds, and entire libraries rest in the palms of our hands. Consider the internet: a global network that democratizes access to information, enables instantaneous communication, and fosters creativity. Never before in human history has so much knowledge been so readily accessible to so many people.

The sheer volume of information available to us today is staggering. At any moment, we can learn about quantum physics, master a new language, or delve into ancient history—all from the comfort of our homes. This ease of access to information is unparalleled and has become a powerful tool for self-improvement, education, and empowerment.

Moreover, technology has broken down barriers that once isolated individuals. Someone in rural Montana can discuss philosophy with someone in Tokyo in real time. This connectivity has fostered a global exchange of ideas, making cultural and intellectual growth a shared endeavor. It's a phenomenon that has arguably brought us closer to understanding humanity's shared aspirations and challenges.

Beyond communication, technology has revolutionized industries. From automated manufacturing to precision agriculture, technological advancements have made it possible to produce more with less, alleviating scarcity in unprecedented ways. While challenges persist in distributing these benefits equitably, the potential for eradicating hunger and poverty is within reach, thanks to modern tools and innovations. The advancements in renewable energy, for instance, hint at a future where sustainable living is not just a possibility but a standard.

A Musical Renaissance

Another triumph of modernity lies in the abundance of music. From streaming platforms to independent artists distributing their work online, we live in an age where every conceivable genre, mood, and cultural expression is available at our fingertips. A listener can transition from Bach to a Mongolian throat-singing ensemble to the latest indie rock single in a matter of moments. Music, one of the most profound forms of human expression, has never been more accessible.

Historically, enjoying diverse music required proximity to live performances or access to expensive recordings. Today, however, technology ensures that anyone with an internet connection can experience the world's auditory treasures. This democratization of music has allowed countless artists to reach audiences they could never have imagined, enriching our lives with sounds that challenge, soothe, and inspire.

Streaming services have not only widened access but also enabled personalized discovery. Algorithms introduce listeners to genres and artists they might never have encountered otherwise, creating an ecosystem where the obscure can flourish alongside the mainstream. For many, music is a lifeline—a source of connection and solace in a world that can often feel overwhelming. The ability to curate personalized soundtracks to our lives is a gift of modern society that should not be taken for granted. It also underscores a broader point: modern society offers us tools to find meaning and connection in ways that previous generations could scarcely imagine.

The Expansion of Knowledge

In previous eras, the accumulation of knowledge was a privilege of the elite. The printing press and subsequent literacy movements began to chip away at this exclusivity, but even then, access was limited. Today, a child with a smartphone has access to more information than a scholar at the Library of Alexandria.

This wealth of knowledge has catalyzed revolutions in science, medicine, and social justice. Global movements advocating for equality and environmental sustainability have been powered by a well-informed populace. Ideas no longer remain confined to ivory towers; they spread and evolve within the collective consciousness.

It's worth noting, however, that such access requires critical thinking. While the abundance of information can empower, it can also overwhelm or mislead. This caveat—the necessity of discernment—will undoubtedly be explored in later chapters, but for now, the focus remains on the unprecedented potential this access provides.

Education, too, has been transformed by modernity. Online courses and open educational resources have made learning more accessible than ever before. The walls of traditional institutions no longer define who can learn; anyone with an internet connection can acquire new skills, sparking a cultural shift that values lifelong learning. For instance, aspiring writers, musicians, or programmers can now access free or affordable resources to hone their crafts, leveling the playing field in ways unimaginable a century ago.

Health and Longevity

Another undeniable success of modern society is the advancement in health care and life expectancy. Vaccines, antibiotics, and improved sanitation have saved countless lives. Diseases that once ravaged populations are now treatable or preventable. Surgical techniques and medical technologies have extended lifespans and improved the quality of life for millions.

While no system is without flaws, the progress made in public health over the last century is remarkable. Compare the life expectancy of today to that of a few centuries ago: where famine, plague, and injury claimed lives prematurely, modern health care offers hope and recovery.

Mental health, once stigmatized and neglected, is now gaining the attention it deserves. While challenges remain, the growing acceptance and availability of mental health care are signs of a society beginning to address the complexities of human well-being holistically. Telemedicine has also made health care more accessible, breaking geographical barriers and ensuring that even remote communities can receive critical medical attention.

A World of Opportunity

Finally, modern society's framework has fostered opportunities for personal growth and expression. While this book will later critique how these opportunities are distributed, it's important to recognize their existence. Today, more individuals have the freedom to pursue careers, passions, and ideas that align with their personal values. Whether it's through formal education, entrepreneurial ventures, or artistic pursuits, modern society encourages—at least in theory—the exploration of potential.

Platforms that allow individuals to share their stories, talents, or businesses with a global audience have created a culture of innovation and self-expression. Someone in a small town can now publish a novel, sell handmade goods, or teach an online course to an audience spanning continents. The gig economy, despite its flaws, has empowered many to take control of their work-life balance, enabling a level of autonomy that past generations might have envied.

Moreover, the rise of social awareness has prompted businesses and institutions to prioritize diversity and inclusion. While far from perfect, these efforts represent a shift towards recognizing and valuing the unique contributions of all individuals. Such progress, however incremental, deserves acknowledgment. Similarly, global travel and multicultural exposure have enriched lives, breaking down prejudices and fostering mutual understanding.

The Balance of Praise and Critique

Acknowledging these positives is not an attempt to romanticize the modern era. Instead, it sets the stage for the nuanced critique that follows. A house may have a sturdy foundation, but that does not mean it's immune to termites or structural flaws. Similarly, while modern society has achieved extraordinary feats, it's far from perfect. By understanding what works—and why—we can better address what doesn't.

As you turn the page, prepare to delve into the perils that accompany these advancements. For every boon of technology, there's a bane. For every connection forged, a disconnect looms. But here, at the outset, let us not forget: humanity was doomed to fail, from the very beginning. History is always repeating. A cycle that never ends? Are we set to fail? The final question I have for you is, how do we break the cycle?

Chapter 2: The Cycle of Sonic Excess

Was it melodramatic to end the previous chapter with such foreboding questions? "Humanity was doomed to fail, from the very beginning. History is always repeating. A cycle that never ends? Are we set to fail? The final question I have for you is, how do we break the cycle?" Perhaps. But who doesn't enjoy a little theatrics every now and then? If anything, I'd argue it was a fitting prelude to this chapter—a chapter that, admittedly, may induce a sense of nausea at the sheer volume of over-analysis it's about to unleash. So grab a coffee or perhaps a stiff drink. Let's talk about the endless loop of consumption and greed, and how we've spun ourselves into an overwhelming cacophony of sonic excess.

A Life Drenched in Noise

Take a moment to reflect on the soundtrack of modern life. Not the intentional one—the playlists we curate, the podcasts we binge, or the ambient rain sounds we use to sleep—but the unending hum of existence itself. Everywhere you go, there is something demanding your attention: a commercial on a gas pump screen, the notification chime of a phone, the din of a public space filled with overlapping conversations. Even silence has become an elusive luxury, a rare commodity in this era of perpetual noise.

This saturation of sound is emblematic of a deeper issue: the unrelenting cycle of consumerism that underpins our modern reality. Every beep, buzz, and jingle is a reminder to buy, subscribe, upgrade, or desire. It's an assault not just on our ears but on our psyche, a constant reinforcement of the idea that what we have will never be enough. We are drenched in noise—sonic and psychological—designed to erode our contentment and spur us toward the next purchase, the next upgrade, the next momentary fix.

Yet, this isn't just about the literal noise. The concept of "sonic excess" goes deeper, symbolizing the overwhelming sensory and emotional input modern society thrusts upon us. It's the cacophony of advertisements that make false promises of happiness, the barrage of choices that paralyze rather than empower, and the unyielding pace of consumption that leaves no room for reflection. We're not just hearing too much; we're feeling too much, thinking too little, and losing ourselves in the process.

Have We Always Been Like This?

Is this relentless consumption—this insatiable hunger for more—hardwired into human nature, or is it a byproduct of careful conditioning? Did ancient humans long for a newer, sleeker stone tool the moment they carved the first one? Or did this mindset arise when societies began to accumulate wealth and surplus, birthing systems of trade, hierarchy, and competition? The answer, like most things, is probably both.

Humans, by nature, are problem solvers. We innovate, adapt, and seek improvement. In many ways, this is our greatest strength. But when this drive is married to systems of profit and power, it mutates into something else entirely: greed. Greed is not mere survival; it's hoarding for hoarding's sake, a desire to dominate and consume beyond reason or necessity. And here's the kicker: the modern world doesn't just tolerate greed—it celebrates it. It slaps a golden bow on it, brands it as ambition, and parades it as the pinnacle of human achievement.

Think of the way society venerates billionaires. They are portrayed not as the apex of greed but as visionaries, innovators, and saviors. Their excess is rarely questioned; it's admired. Meanwhile, the systems they uphold—systems that exploit workers, devastate the environment, and perpetuate inequality—are treated as inevitable or even virtuous. This normalization of greed isn't human nature. It's human nurture, carefully cultivated over centuries by those who benefit most from its perpetuation.

The Careful Nurturing of Greed

Let's not pretend this is all accidental. Consumer culture didn't just happen; it was designed. From Edward Bernays' pioneering use of psychology in advertising to the rise of planned obsolescence, every aspect of modern life has been meticulously engineered to ensure we keep consuming. Bernays, the so-called father of public relations, weaponized Freud's theories of the unconscious to link products to desires that ran deeper than utility. Cigarettes became symbols of freedom; cars became extensions of identity. The result? A society so entangled in the web of consumption that it can scarcely imagine life outside it.

Products are no longer built to last because durability is bad for business. Instead, we are sold the illusion of choice, a smorgasbord of nearly identical options that feed the same ravenous machine. Consider the smartphone. It's arguably one of the most revolutionary tools ever created, yet it's also a shining example of this cycle. Every year, a new model is unveiled with incremental upgrades and a hefty price tag.

And every year, millions of perfectly functional devices are discarded in favor of the "next big thing." Why? Because we've been conditioned to equate newness with value and obsolescence with failure.

The same pattern plays out in countless industries. Fashion cycles through trends at breakneck speed, ensuring that last season's wardrobe is this season's faux pas. Streaming services battle for dominance by flooding the market with content, much of it forgettable, yet all of it demanding our precious time and attention. Even food has fallen prey to this cycle, with "limited edition" flavors and Instagram-worthy gimmicks designed to create a sense of urgency around consumption. The market demands an endless appetite, and we oblige.

Sonic Excess: The Soundtrack of Greed

Nowhere is this culture of excess more apparent than in our relationship with sound. Music, once a deeply personal and communal experience, has become another commodity to be consumed in endless quantities. Streaming platforms boast libraries of tens of millions of songs, yet how many of us truly savor what we listen to? Instead, we skip, shuffle, and scroll—always searching for the next track, the next hit of dopamine.

Even the act of discovery has been commodified. Algorithms serve us playlists tailored to our preferences, reducing the thrill of finding something new to a sterile transaction. And while this convenience is undoubtedly a marvel of modern technology, it also raises uncomfortable questions. Are we truly choosing what we listen to, or are we being guided by invisible hands toward what is most profitable? Is our taste our own, or has it been shaped by the relentless churn of the industry?

Sonic excess goes beyond mere sound; it's the relentless layering of distraction upon distraction, a fog of noise designed to drown out critical thought. It numbs us, dulls our awareness, and leaves us vulnerable to suggestion. The irony is almost poetic: in a world where we have more access to music than ever before, we've never been less attuned to it.

The Psychological Weight of Noise

The psychological impact of this noise cannot be overstated. Studies have shown that constant exposure to advertising and media not only increases stress levels but also erodes self-esteem. When every message tells you that you're lacking—that you need this product, this lifestyle, this experience to be whole—it's impossible not to internalize some of that negativity. Over time, this creates a population that is not just willing but desperate to consume, mistaking consumption for fulfillment.

Philosophically, this raises profound questions about the nature of happiness and the human condition. Are we truly better off for all our advancements, or have we simply found more sophisticated ways to distract ourselves from existential despair? Ancient philosophers like Epicurus believed that happiness lay in simplicity, in the absence of unnecessary desires. Modern society seems to have taken the opposite approach, equating happiness with the fulfillment of endless wants. But can a want ever truly be fulfilled, or does its satisfaction only give birth to new desires?

Breaking the Cycle

If all of this sounds bleak, that's because it is. But acknowledging the problem is the first step toward solving it. To break free from this cycle of consumption and excess, we must first recognize its grip on our lives. This isn't easy. It requires confronting uncomfortable truths about ourselves and the systems we participate in. It means asking hard questions about what we value and why.

Do we really need the newest gadget, the trendiest outfit, or the latest streaming subscription? Or are we chasing these things because we've been taught to equate them with happiness and success? Breaking the cycle doesn't mean rejecting modernity outright. It means reclaiming our agency within it. It means making conscious choices about what we consume and why.

The Path Forward

As we move through this book, these questions will become increasingly pressing. For now, let us sit with discomfort. Let us acknowledge the ways in which we've been complicit in perpetuating this cycle, even as we critique it. And let us remember that change, while difficult, is always possible. After all, history may repeat itself, and unfortunately you cannot change that. Or can you?

Chapter 3: The Subscription Loop

Subscriptions: the ultimate symbol of modern life's seamless convenience, yet the embodiment of endless complexity. In a world dominated by immediate access and digital consumption, subscriptions have become an inescapable fixture of our existence. They promise to streamline our lives, offering us everything from entertainment to services with little more than a click. Yet, the more we subscribe, the more we realize that we're trapped in an endless loop—consumed by convenience, but devoid of control. What begins as a promise of simplicity is revealed to be a paradox: an illusion of freedom that pulls us deeper into the web of consumerism.

In this chapter, we will explore the subscribed life, peeling back its glossy surface to reveal the deeper contradictions at play. Through this exploration, we uncover not only the moral and existential consequences of subscription culture but also the ways it shapes our sense of self, our relationships with ownership, and the very nature of consumption.

The License You Didn't Ask For

When we think about purchasing something in the digital age, we tend to assume that ownership is part of the deal. Buy a song from iTunes, download a movie from Amazon, or purchase an e-book from Kindle, and you expect, at least in theory, that these items are yours to keep and enjoy forever. And for a time, that was true. For a while, buying a digital good felt almost identical to purchasing a physical item. You made a transaction, you received a file, and you were free to access it whenever you wanted. But digital ownership is an illusion—one that becomes painfully clear when your purchased content is suddenly gone.

This is the paradox of the "digital purchase." Yes, you paid for a movie, but did you truly own it? No. What you own is a license—an ephemeral right to access the content under certain conditions, and that license can expire or be revoked at any time, without warning or recourse. The content is always at the mercy of its distributor. A beloved film could vanish from your library overnight, swept away by licensing disputes, corporate mergers, or content rights being sold off to a competitor.

It's a strange feeling, isn't it? To watch something you "bought" disappear, to have a product you thought was yours vanish with a few clicks of a mouse. You might be refunded, or offered a similar product as a replacement, but the experience doesn't feel the same. The loss isn't just financial—it's a loss of control. You never truly owned the film or the song, and with that realization comes a chilling sense of helplessness. The ownership of digital goods, once seen as a future-facing utopia, has instead become an endless cycle of renting, where the true power lies with the corporation.

The Illusion of Physical Media

At first, physical media may seem like the solution to this digital dilemma. To purchase a tangible item—whether a DVD, vinyl record, or Blu-ray disc—seems to offer something more permanent, more real. You own the object. You can display it, use it, and most importantly, it won't vanish from your collection without a trace. No mysterious glitches, no licensing conflicts. Or so we tell ourselves.

However, once we scratch the surface of physical media, the cracks begin to show. The idea that physical media offers "true ownership" is, in itself, a myth. Sure, you can physically possess the object, but with every new format, every "definitive" edition, every box set, the same question arises: why do you need to buy the same thing again? The answer is always the same: the new version has something "better"—a clearer image, a special feature, or a piece of artwork that makes it more collectible. We're encouraged to constantly upgrade, to replace our old collections with the "latest and greatest," all while the previous versions become obsolete.

In this way, physical media mirrors digital consumption: it's a cycle of endless upgrading and disposal. There's always a new version to buy, always something more complete, more polished, and more exclusive. What was once "owned" is now just another object in the churn of consumerism—still existing, but ultimately replaceable and fleeting.

Then, there's the environmental cost. To produce, package, and ship physical media requires resources—raw materials, plastics, transportation—and these all contribute to a growing ecological footprint. The process of printing, pressing, and distributing physical media is far from eco-friendly. Yet, the "ownership" of that shiny vinyl record or Blu-ray disc comes with no acknowledgment of the ecological consequences, nor any real sense of permanence beyond our personal collection. The very object that is marketed as a symbol of real ownership becomes a part of a disposable, wasteful system.

The Greedy Hydra of Subscriptions

While the debate between digital and physical media rages on, there's an even more pervasive force in modern life: subscriptions. These services, which began as a way to streamline access to entertainment and services, have quickly morphed into the defining feature of modern consumerism. They're a hydra, sprouting endless heads, each offering a seemingly endless variety of goods, services, and experiences—all for the low price of a monthly fee. What began as the promise of convenient access has now become a tangled web of fees, each one demanding a piece of your income.

The subscription model has transformed everything—from media to food to software—into something you rent rather than own. Need a movie? Subscribe to Netflix or

Amazon Prime. Need music? Spotify or Apple Music has you covered. Need groceries? Well, now you can subscribe to meal delivery kits, which will send fresh ingredients to your door every week. Software? Adobe Creative Cloud. Office Suite? Microsoft 365. The options are endless, but with each subscription you sign up for, your life becomes more and more entangled in the web of constant consumption.

This is the true nature of the subscription model: fragmentation. No longer can you rely on a single service to meet all of your needs. To satisfy your entertainment needs, you need multiple subscriptions—Hulu for TV shows, Netflix for original series, Disney+ for Marvel and Star Wars, and Amazon Prime for convenience and the occasional documentary. But no one service offers everything you need, and so you are left juggling multiple subscriptions—each one a new entity to monitor, maintain, and keep up with.

Meanwhile, the subscription model thrives on the illusion of convenience. It's sold to us under the guise of "flexibility." No more long-term commitments. No more contracts. Just pay for what you use and cancel when you're done. But in reality, it's a vicious cycle. As one subscription ends, another begins. There's always something new to subscribe to, a new service that promises to fulfill your needs, whether it's a new fitness app, a curated fashion box, or a subscription to premium content from your favorite YouTuber.

The irony of the subscription model is this: it was meant to free us from the clutter of ownership, but it has created an entirely new form of enslavement. We are chained not by physical objects, but by an ongoing, invisible obligation to maintain access to services we may not even need anymore. The more subscriptions we sign up for, the more fragmented our lives become, until we are left with a sense of emptiness, as if we're drowning in a sea of options, none of which feel permanent or fulfilling.

A Three-Way War of Greed

The contradictions inherent in these consumption models come into sharp focus when we consider the constant battle between three competing visions: digital ownership, physical media, and subscriptions. Each of these forces pulls in different directions, each promising its own form of freedom, each casting the other as inferior.

The first voice, championing digital ownership, argues that the future lies in accessible, downloadable content. Digital files are more efficient, more environmentally friendly, and more flexible. You can take them anywhere, store them in the cloud, and never worry about losing a physical copy. However, this voice is undercut by the fragility of digital ownership. Sure, you own the file, but as soon as that file becomes inaccessible—whether through a licensing conflict or a service shutdown—you are left with nothing but an empty promise.

The second voice, defending physical media, insists that true ownership comes only through tangible, physical artifacts. These objects are permanent. They have value that transcends their functionality, offering not just entertainment, but a sense of pride and nostalgia. But physical media, too, has its flaws. It's bulky, it requires space, and it contributes to waste. More importantly, it's constantly being replaced by newer, better versions—each one marketing itself as the "ultimate edition" of what you once thought was a perfect item.

The third voice, representing the subscription model, insists that the future lies not in owning things, but in having access. Why own a physical DVD or a digital file when you can have it all, at any time, with a single payment? Subscriptions promise convenience, flexibility, and the joy of endless choices. But these too come with a price: the loss of permanence, the endless churn of content that is ultimately fleeting and unsubstantial.

Each voice has its flaws, and none offer a perfect solution. But they all speak to the same truth: ownership, in all its forms, is becoming increasingly illusory. In a world of digital licenses, remasters, and subscriptions, we are left with a strange new reality—one in which we are constantly consuming but never truly possessing.

The Psychological Toll of Subscriptions

As we navigate this tangled web of consumption, we must confront the psychological toll it takes. Subscription culture does not just change the way we consume; it reshapes how we relate to the world around us. Subscriptions promise access, but they also encourage an unhealthy dependency. We're no longer free to choose; we're constantly bombarded with options, forced to make decisions not based on what we truly want, but on what is available to us at the moment.

This constant consumption undermines our ability to feel truly fulfilled. We're always chasing the next big thing—the next series to binge, the next album to listen to, the next service to try. But this cycle of endless consumption leaves us feeling hollow. We are always waiting for something new, but in the process, we never have the chance to fully appreciate what we already have.

We are also taught to value access over ownership. In a world where everything is just a subscription away, we stop thinking about the long-term. Instead, we're encouraged to live in the moment, to consume whatever is at hand. We stop asking ourselves whether we need something, and instead ask whether it's available to us now. We are driven not by desire, but by convenience.

This constant churn of consumption also creates a sense of dissatisfaction. We are no longer able to hold onto things. Whether digital or physical, everything is transient. The things we once valued—whether a movie we cherished or a song that once meant something—are now fleeting, consumed in the blink of an eye and discarded just as quickly.

The Contradiction Within the Page: The Book Itself as a Paradox

As we delve deeper into the concepts outlined within this book, one undeniable truth becomes clear: this very book exists as a contradiction to everything it sets out to explain. In the course of writing it, I've been forced to confront the paradox at the heart of this entire endeavor. For all its analysis of consumerism, the digital age, and the illusion of ownership, the act of creating this book becomes, in itself, a point of confusion—a paradox wrapped in layers of irony.

Here I am, writing about the falseness of ownership, the emptiness of endless consumption, and the consequences of our subscription-based lives, all while offering you—dear reader—a book that, by its very nature, is an object of consumption. You're reading my words, and in doing so, you've subscribed—whether consciously or not—to the experience of this book. By purchasing or downloading it, you've engaged in a transaction, and suddenly the very idea of freedom and ownership that this book seeks to explore becomes muddled. You've traded money (or time, or attention) for a thing that, once read, you can never "unread"—a piece of content that will forever exist in your mind, yet still, in some way, belongs to me, the author, as part of my intellectual property.

In other words, in the very process of deconstructing the false narratives of ownership, I've unknowingly contributed to them. How can I, as the writer of this book, claim to be rejecting the very notion of ownership and consumption when the entire act of creating this book involves you consuming something that I've authored and published for the sole purpose of having you consume it? The paradox is undeniable: to write a book about rejecting consumption and ownership is to simultaneously perpetuate the very cycle it critiques.

Let's pause for a moment and reflect on what's happening here. As you read, you're bound to engage with these ideas—ideas that, in themselves, undermine the very medium through which they're delivered. It's an odd, almost self-defeating exercise. I tell you that subscription culture, digital goods, and the fleeting nature of ownership are all problematic. I show you how we are trapped in an endless loop of consumption and "temporary possession." Yet, as you progress through this text, I am contributing to that very cycle. I have, in essence, asked you to participate in the act of consuming this book, to take it as your own, even though the ideas within it directly critique the way we consume things in the first place.

This realization adds a layer of confusion to the mix. It's as though I'm both pulling the rug out from under you and inviting you to sit down on it. I'm inviting you into a world of thought that pushes against the very systems of consumption, but I'm doing it through the medium that embodies those systems. And in that sense, writing this book becomes a bit like trying to escape a maze by running in circles—it's inherently flawed, self-aware, and tangled in contradictions.

I am also confronted by the strange reality that, despite all the arguments I make in these pages against endless consumption, my motivations in writing this book are no different from those I criticize. I want you to read it. I want you to subscribe, in a way, to the experience of it, to engage with these ideas, and perhaps even to agree with them. But in doing so, I am participating in the very act of promotion and self-promotion that I am railing against. I have created something for you to consume, to consider, to share, to buy, to download, to hold—even if only for a moment. And that makes me just another cog in the machine, another player in the game I set out to critique. It's a bizarre, almost laughable contradiction: to critique a system while simultaneously living within it, to point out the flaws of ownership while holding onto the intellectual property I created.

Perhaps you, too, are caught in this paradox. You might find yourself agreeing with the points raised in these pages—recognizing the contradictions in the modern consumerist mindset, acknowledging the absurdity of subscription culture, the emptiness of transient ownership—but as you engage with this text, you are drawn into the very paradox that it exposes. You may question the validity of the ideas presented, wondering how they can possibly be true if the author, who is presenting them, is engaging in the same behaviors. It's a valid concern, and one that I have wrestled with throughout the process of writing this book.

But this contradiction is not merely an intellectual oversight or an unfortunate flaw in the execution. Rather, it is a central, unavoidable element of the conversation. To write about the flawed nature of consumption is to embody that flaw. To speak out against the transient nature of ownership is to acknowledge that my own work is, itself, a product of this transience. The very act of writing about it makes it part of the very cycle I'm trying to dissect. The book is both a commentary on and an embodiment of the very forces it critiques.

This contradiction is compounded when we consider the act of writing itself. How can I, as a writer, claim to provide clarity on these issues when the act of writing—of shaping, crafting, and packaging my thoughts into this book—only contributes to the noise of a world already saturated with content? I'm adding to the sea of information, filling the space with more words, more noise, more ideas that are only one click away from being discarded, one subscription away from fading into obscurity.

I cannot escape the fact that writing this book is, in itself, a form of subscription. Once you engage with it, you are in it, whether you agree with it or not. You are bound to the words on these pages, even as you become aware that they are part of a system that thrives on consumption, repetition, and endless engagement. The book is designed for you to keep reading, to reflect, to react, to engage in the conversation. And yet, with each word, with each page, we further entrench ourselves in the very cycle I am attempting to critique.

It's a beautiful, maddening paradox—one that forces us to question whether we can ever truly escape the systems we critique. Can we truly remove ourselves from the machinery of consumption? Or, is the act of questioning these systems just another way of feeding them, of giving them more to consume? I've raised these questions in this book, but in doing so, I've already placed you, the reader, into the very web I've tried to untangle.

So, as you continue reading, as you continue consuming this text, remember that it is a product of the very culture I am discussing—a contradiction, an irony, a piece of work that refuses to be free of the very forces it critiques. In that way, this book becomes not just an examination of the contradictions of ownership and consumption, but an embodiment of them. It is a piece of content, a part of the very system that we are all trapped within. And in that, it offers its own kind of commentary: that there may be no way out, no final escape from the cycle of consumption. We can point out the flaws, we can critique them, but in the end, we are still part of the machine.

The End of the Road

Ultimately, the subscribed life leads to one inescapable conclusion: we are all living in a kind of perpetual present. Our lives are reduced to a series of short-term commitments, each one promising convenience, but never offering the fulfillment that true ownership—or even true freedom—can bring. In a world where everything is available on demand, we find ourselves with less and less to hold on to. The promise of access is not freedom, but the illusion of freedom—a paradox that we, willingly or unwillingly, continue to embrace.

As we stand on the edge of this new reality, the question remains: will we ever truly own anything again? Or will we forever be stuck in the cycle of consumption, chasing after the next subscription, the next piece of content, only to realize that we never really had it in the first place?

In the end, the subscribed life is not one of freedom, but one of endless consumption. We are all players in a game we didn't choose—one where ownership is no longer possible, and control is but a fleeting illusion.

Chapter 4: The Liberation of Doing Nothing

In modern society, the constant hum of productivity drowns out the stillness of the present. The pressure to always be doing, always moving, always *progressing* is suffocating. We're conditioned to believe that nothing is worth doing unless it has a purpose, a goal, or an outcome that feeds the insatiable hunger of a world built on consumption and achievement. But here's the thing: no one is actually enjoying any of it. Everyone is in a perpetual state of motion, caught in a cycle of consumption and production, and yet no one is *living*.

We are trapped in a world that tells us we must always be doing something. Every moment must be accounted for, every decision must lead somewhere. But somewhere along the way, we've lost sight of something simple—something pure. What if the greatest act of defiance, the most revolutionary thing you could do in this world, was to stop? To do nothing. No goals, no ambition, no checklist. Just a moment of stillness, of being, of existing without purpose. But in a society that thrives on constant movement, that's a hard thing to embrace.

The truth is, everyone is exhausted, everyone is trying to stay ahead in a race that has no finish line. People work themselves to the bone, burn out, and fall into the trap of constantly needing to achieve something in order to feel validated. They forget that nothing, truly nothing, has to be about achievement. This obsession with doing has stolen something from us. We've forgotten the beauty of simply existing, of just taking a breath and observing the world without the pressure to *be* something, *do* something, *achieve* something.

But here's where it gets difficult. Because even now, as I'm writing this, I am caught in the act of doing. I am creating something with words, trying to articulate this feeling of stillness, when all I really want to say is: stop. And I realize the irony of this. Writing this chapter is exactly the kind of behavior I'm criticizing. I'm playing into the same cycle of trying to make sense of everything, trying to find meaning in every action, even when the answer is to just *be*. But in this contradiction, perhaps the lesson lies. We are always, at some level, part of the machine. Even when we try to stop, the world around us is relentless, pushing us to move, pushing us to do more. But the very act of stopping, of saying "no" to that pressure, is an act of rebellion.

The Tyranny of Constant Movement

From the moment we wake up, we are in motion. Our minds are filled with lists of tasks, deadlines, expectations. We're taught to fill every gap of time with something—anything—to keep the gears of society turning. Take a break? That's for the weak. Rest? That's a luxury only the rich can afford. No, we must hustle. We must work. We must strive. The idea of sitting still, doing nothing, seems like a crime against progress.

But the problem isn't that we're busy—it's that we don't know how to stop. We don't know how to just *exist*. To look out the window without needing to check our phones. To take a walk without an agenda. To just sit in a chair, stare at the ceiling, and do nothing. And *nothing* doesn't have to be a bad thing. In fact, it's in that nothingness that we can find liberation.

There's a strange irony in all of this: by constantly moving, constantly reacting, constantly consuming, we think we're living, but we're only existing in a loop. We're not experiencing life; we're surviving it, waiting for the next thing to give us some fleeting satisfaction. But what if that moment of satisfaction could come from nothing? What if the answer to the chaos was not more action but more stillness?

The Gift of Doing Nothing

Take a day off, and I mean *a real* day off. No work, no emails, no meetings. Stop moving, stop reacting, stop trying to make everything into something. In that emptiness, you'll find clarity. In the quiet, you'll discover something that's been buried under the noise: a sense of peace, a return to yourself. That's the liberation we've all forgotten how to access.

It's so simple, yet so radical. Doing nothing is often viewed as an act of rebellion. The world tells us that every moment must be filled with purpose, and if we're not producing, we're wasting our time. But perhaps the truest act of rebellion is to just be still. To do nothing. It is in that stillness where we can reconnect with the most basic, human part of ourselves.

Doing nothing doesn't mean wasting time. It doesn't mean you've failed to make the most of your life. It means you've stepped off the hamster wheel for a moment, and in doing so, you've gained something more valuable than any product or achievement: your own time, your own space, your own presence. It's a form of self-care, a form of freedom.

One thing my father taught me was the importance of slowing down, of simply taking a breath and appreciating the moment. There were countless times I'd get caught up in something—work, school, life—and he'd tell me, "Boy, you need to calm down. Not everything needs to be a race. Sometimes, the most important thing you can do is nothing at all. Just sit there and be. Everything else will fall into place when it's time." I didn't understand it at first, and maybe it was because I was too young, too focused on the idea of success, of always moving forward. But now, I realize the wisdom in his words. It's a gift to do nothing, to let go of the endless striving for a moment and just *exist*.

In fact, it was through my father that I was introduced to the teachings of Alan Watts. My father, always a thinker, would often play Watts' lectures in the background as we went about our nightly chats. "You're so caught up in what you're trying to achieve," he would say to me, quoting Watts. "But the real magic happens when you stop trying so hard." I didn't get it at the time, of course, but looking back, those words have stuck with me. Alan Watts, in his uniquely philosophical and accessible style, often spoke about the idea of "letting go" and living in the present moment. He talked about how people spend their lives either looking back at the past or obsessing over the future, never appreciating the present, the only time that truly exists. His words resonated, even though I didn't fully understand them at the time. The present moment—this one right here—is all we really have. And yet, we spend so much of our time trying to avoid it, constantly looking ahead or behind.

The Paradox of Productivity

Here's where it gets tricky: even writing this chapter, as I'm reflecting on the need for stillness, is inherently contradictory. In my attempt to describe the beauty of doing nothing, I am, in fact, doing something. I'm engaging in the very cycle I'm criticizing. This book itself is a perfect example of the paradox at the heart of modern life. It's about the quest for meaning, but by writing it, I am adding to the very noise I'm trying to quiet.

It's a paradox I can't escape. Every word I type goes against the core message of this chapter. I'm speaking about the virtue of stillness, but still, I'm moving forward, trying to make a point, trying to be productive. This book, in its essence, is a contradiction. It is a meditation on the absurdity of progress and productivity, yet it is born out of my own drive to communicate something, to make something meaningful out of this. By writing this, I am feeding into the very system I'm critiquing.

It's a reminder that there is no clean resolution in this pursuit. We are all part of the machine. We are both the creators and the products, trapped in the cycle of progress, of doing. But that's the absurdity of modern life. We can talk about stopping, about doing nothing, but we will always find ourselves moving again, pushing forward, reacting to the world around us.

The Cigarette Analogy

There's an analogy I once heard, and it's one that sticks with me because it's so simple, yet so profound. People who smoke—there's always a part of the conversation where they talk about quitting. "I should quit," they say. "I know I need to quit," they say, as they light up yet another cigarette. But why do they keep saying they need to quit? Why don't they just shut the fuck up for a moment, inhale, and enjoy the cigarette? It's not about the cigarette itself—it's about the constant mental noise, the constant tension, the pressure to stop doing something that gives them even the slightest amount of satisfaction. It's like everyone is always thinking they need to stop doing something to be better, to be more efficient, to be more aligned with some idea of "success," but they never actually stop to appreciate what's happening right now. Why not stop and just *enjoy* the moment?

I'm paraphrasing here, but the point is clear: what are we so afraid of? People say they want to quit smoking so they can live another eight years, just so they can keep buying Amazon products and getting caught up in a consumer-driven society that never gives them real happiness? What is the point? What are we really working toward? If the only goal is more years of trying to fill the void with stuff—more purchases, more work, more consumption—then what is the difference between being here or gone?

The world tells us we need to quit, we need to strive for something better. But maybe the real question is: *Why*? Why should we keep trying to fit into a mold that doesn't serve us? Maybe it's time to stop and ask ourselves if the pursuit of more is even worth it.

The Perils of Modern Life

And there lies the issue. We're so obsessed with progress, with moving forward, with improving ourselves in every possible way, that we miss the point of it all. Everyone's caught in a trap, constantly trying to change themselves into something they think they're supposed to be. But no one is ever satisfied, because there's always something else to improve, something else to do. And here's the thing: that cycle is endless. The more we strive to *fix* ourselves, the more we distance ourselves from the very thing we're looking for: peace. Fulfillment. Stillness.

This is why we need to stop. Not just physically, but mentally. The continuous chatter in our heads about what we should be doing, where we should be going, how we should be improving—it's exhausting. It's like trying to solve a puzzle that was never meant to be solved. It's like trying to complete a task that has no end. And in that perpetual striving, we never give ourselves the space to just *be*. But when we step away from that constant cycle, when we give ourselves permission to just exist, we find a kind of peace we never thought was possible.

This is something my father taught me. He's always had a way of cutting through the noise. I can remember countless times when I'd be stressed, overthinking everything, and he'd look at me with a calmness I could never quite grasp and say, "Just stop. You're not going anywhere by running around in circles. Take a moment. Relax. Let it all go." He taught me that sometimes the best thing you can do is nothing at all. Sometimes, the greatest act of self-care is stepping back and letting the world spin without you for a while.

And this is where Alan Watts comes in. My father first introduced me to his lectures when I was young, and though I didn't fully understand them at the time, I now see how profound they were. Watts often spoke about the need to "let go" of the need to control everything. He talked about the difference between living life with awareness and simply reacting to it. He described life as a dance—a rhythm that flows naturally if you stop forcing your steps. The more you try to control, the more you disrupt the flow. But when you step back, stop forcing it, and just *be*, you move with the rhythm of life rather than against it.

Watts' philosophy mirrored what my father had been teaching me for years. "You don't need to fix everything," he'd say. "You don't need to 'achieve' anything in order to be worthwhile. You already are." My father made me realize that life isn't about adding more layers of productivity or achievement, it's about stripping away the noise and just experiencing the moment. In this way, I began to understand that happiness doesn't come from doing more; it comes from doing less.

The Pressure to Do

But the world we live in is designed to make us feel like we're never enough. We're conditioned to believe that we always need to be doing more, that success is tied to our constant productivity. It's exhausting. Everyone is caught in the rat race, chasing after something they can't quite define. And when they reach one goal, there's always another waiting just beyond it. The pressure is relentless. The constant need to be doing, achieving, advancing—it never stops. But the question I ask is: what's the point?

At the end of it all, does it matter how many hours you've worked, how many things you've acquired, or how much you've progressed in your career? Will it really matter if you miss the present moment in your relentless pursuit of the future? The fact is, we're all running toward something, but few of us know what that something is. We just know we can't stop. But if we did stop, even for a moment, we might realize that the thing we were running toward was right in front of us all along.

And in a world so obsessed with efficiency, with getting things done, we forget that true peace is found in the opposite: in surrender, in letting go of the need to control, in simply existing without pressure. The beauty of life lies in the moments that aren't planned, the moments that aren't structured or measured. These are the moments when we truly live.

An Uncomfortable Truth

But I won't lie to you—it's uncomfortable. To stop, to do nothing, feels wrong in a world that tells you it's lazy or unproductive. But that discomfort is the first sign of liberation. It's like the first moment you realize that you've been holding your breath your whole life, and now, for the first time, you can finally exhale. The very act of letting go is terrifying, because it means stepping outside of everything you've been taught about how life should be lived.

But that's where freedom lies. In letting go. In doing nothing. It's in the moments of stillness where the noise dies down, and you can finally hear your own thoughts. And that's the gift I've learned to cherish—something my father passed on to me, and something I hope to share with you. The act of stepping back, of doing nothing, is not a retreat or a surrender; it's a reclaiming of the self.

It's ironic, isn't it? Here I am, writing a chapter about the importance of doing nothing, and yet, I'm writing. I'm producing. I'm still part of the system I'm critiquing. But in this very contradiction lies the truth: sometimes, there's no perfect answer. Sometimes, you just have to take a step back, stop judging yourself, and just *be*.

Reclaiming Our Time

So what if we stopped? What if we stopped reacting to everything and started living on our terms? What if we took a day, a week, a month, and just didn't do anything? We could stop buying things we don't need, stop chasing dreams we're not sure are ours, stop trying to prove something to people who don't matter. What if we stopped running? Would we feel liberated? Or would we feel lost, unsure of who we are without the constant need to move?

The world might try to convince us that we're wasting time by doing nothing, but I'd argue that *doing nothing* might be the most meaningful thing we can do. Because in that stillness, we can finally hear what really matters.

So, take a day off. Calm down. Let the world keep spinning while you take a breath and do

absolutely nothing. Maybe it's the only thing
that's worth doing.

Chapter 5: Capitalism's Decline and the Future of America

Capitalism, in the United States, is not merely an economic system; it is a social and political framework that has been molded and shaped over centuries. To truly understand the failures of capitalism, it is vital to revisit its origins in America. The United States was founded on the labor of enslaved Africans and the dispossession of Native Americans, creating a society where profit was built on the backs of those who were systematically oppressed and exploited.

The first European settlers arrived on the shores of North America with the clear intention of establishing a system based on exploitation, seeking to enrich themselves through the labor of indigenous populations and enslaved Africans. The indigenous peoples, who had cultivated and protected the land for centuries, were forcibly removed, massacred, and displaced as European settlers began their colonial expansion. The wealth of European colonial powers was built on the land stolen from Native Americans, and the labor of enslaved Africans, who were brutally torn from their homeland and forced into hard labor to grow the crops and build the economy of the New World.

In *A People's History of the United States*, Howard Zinn describes the founding of America as a system rooted in exploitation: "The settlers came to America with a capitalist mindset, intending to conquer land, resources, and people. Their early economic activity was built on slavery, violence, and the dispossession of native peoples" (Zinn, 1980). It was here, at the very beginning, that the foundations of inequality were set. Capitalism, born out of this violent exploitation, continues to perpetuate a cycle of inequality and wealth concentration that benefits the few at the expense of the many.

This history was not an aberration but the starting point of the American economic system. Early economic policies, such as land grants to wealthy landowners and the establishment of a slave economy in the South, reinforced the belief that profit, not human well-being, should be the guiding principle. This vision of capitalism—one that prioritized property and wealth accumulation over the humanity of people—became ingrained in the national psyche and continues to shape American politics today.

The Industrial Revolution and the Rise of American Capitalism

The transition from an agrarian economy to an industrialized one marked a new chapter in the history of capitalism in America. The Industrial Revolution, beginning in the late 19th century, saw the rise of massive corporations that dominated the economy. The wealth generated by industrialization was staggering, but it was concentrated in the hands of a few elite industrialists, while the vast majority of workers endured poor working conditions, low wages, and a lack of job security.

Figures like Andrew Carnegie and John D. Rockefeller amassed immense fortunes through monopolistic practices, exploiting workers and undermining competition to maintain their grip on the economy. The rise of the corporate class during this period mirrored the same inequality that had characterized earlier periods of American history. As labor unions began to organize in response to the injustices workers faced, the capitalist class used state power to suppress these movements, often through violent means. The Pullman Strike of 1894, where federal troops were called in to crush the labor uprising, is one stark example of how the state and corporate interests worked together to maintain capitalist hegemony.

The Gilded Age, as this period is known, was marked by an immense concentration of wealth, political corruption, and the degradation of the working class. The notion of the "self-made man" was propagated by wealthy industrialists like Carnegie, but this myth obscured the reality that their success was built on the exploitation of others. Workers, particularly immigrants, labored under brutal conditions in factories, mines, and railroads. They were subject to long hours, low pay, and dangerous working environments, all while the wealth generated by their labor flowed into the pockets of the capitalist class.

Capitalism's Crisis in the 20th Century: The Great Depression and the New Deal

The early 20th century saw the first major crisis of capitalism in the United States with the Great Depression of 1929. The stock market crash that began in October of 1929 marked the beginning of a decade-long economic collapse that devastated millions of Americans. Unemployment rates soared, industrial production ground to a halt, and banks failed at unprecedented rates. The failure of the capitalist system was laid bare as millions of people found themselves destitute, struggling to survive in a country that had promised them prosperity.

In *The Great Depression: A Diary*, author Benjamin Roth details the emotional and economic toll of the Great Depression: "For the first time, people understood that capitalism could fail. It was no longer just a philosophical discussion; it was a lived experience" (Roth, 1948). The Great Depression demonstrated that capitalism, when left unchecked, could lead to economic collapse and widespread suffering. In response to this crisis, President Franklin D. Roosevelt introduced the New Deal, a series of programs aimed at providing relief, recovery, and reform. The New Deal was a direct challenge to the laissez-faire capitalism that had dominated the previous decades.

Through measures like Social Security, unemployment insurance, and public works programs, the New Deal sought to provide a safety net for the most vulnerable in society. Roosevelt's reforms also aimed to regulate the financial system, introducing the Securities Exchange Act of 1934 to curb stock market speculation and prevent future crashes. These policies were a direct response to the failure of capitalism to provide for the people, offering a glimpse of what a more equitable economic system might look like.

However, the New Deal was not without its limitations. Despite its ambitious goals, it did not fully dismantle the capitalist system or address the root causes of inequality. While the New Deal helped to alleviate some of the worst effects of the Great Depression, it left the underlying capitalist structures in place. As historian Eric Foner notes in *The Story of American Freedom*, "Roosevelt's reforms were crucial, but they did not challenge the fundamental inequality of wealth in America" (Foner, 1998).

The Reagan Era: The Resurgence of Neoliberal Capitalism

The 1980s saw a resurgence of right-wing economic policies under President Ronald Reagan. Reagan's administration embraced neoliberalism, which advocated for lower taxes, deregulation, and the privatization of public services. Reagan promised that these policies would create prosperity for all, but in practice, they disproportionately benefited the wealthy and corporations. The wealth gap widened, and the middle class stagnated, while Reagan's tax cuts for the rich and deregulation of industries led to a series of corporate scandals and the rise of financial speculation.

In *The Shock Doctrine: The Rise of Disaster Capitalism*, Naomi Klein explains how Reagan's policies were part of a broader global shift toward neoliberalism: "Reagan, Thatcher, and other neoliberal leaders created a world where wealth was redistributed upward, to the richest individuals and corporations, while public services and social safety nets were dismantled" (Klein, 2007). Reagan's policies, including the deregulation of banks and the cutting of social programs, ultimately resulted in the concentration of wealth at the top and the dismantling of the social safety net that had been established during the New Deal.

The long-term consequences of Reagan's policies were far-reaching. The deregulation of industries, particularly in the financial sector, contributed to the savings and loan crisis of the late 1980s and the 2008 financial crisis. Reagan's tax cuts, while initially stimulating economic growth, also resulted in a massive increase in the national debt, as tax revenues plummeted while military spending soared. Reagan's presidency marked the beginning of a shift away from the progressive policies of the New Deal era and toward a more market-driven approach to governance.

Bush Sr. and the Failure of Reaganomics

When George H.W. Bush succeeded Reagan in 1989, he inherited an economy that was in turmoil. While Reagan's tax cuts and military spending had led to a brief period of economic expansion, they had also created an unsustainable national debt. Bush's attempt to continue Reagan's policies, particularly his decision to cut taxes and increase military spending, exacerbated the budget deficit. In *The Great Recession: A Subprime Crisis*, financial analyst Raghuram Rajan explains how the Bush administration's failure to rein in the financial sector led to the housing bubble and eventual financial collapse (Rajan, 2010).

The 1990s saw a return to prosperity under President Bill Clinton, largely due to his more moderate approach, which included deficit reduction and a focus on economic growth through technological innovation. However, Clinton's policies also included deregulation measures, particularly in the financial sector, that contributed to the housing crisis of the mid-2000s. Despite Clinton's successes in reducing the deficit and fostering a period of economic growth, his administration did little to address the structural inequalities within the capitalist system, laying the groundwork for the crisis that would come under George W. Bush.

Bush Jr. and the 2008 Financial Crisis: A Fatal Blow to Capitalism

The 2008 financial crisis marked the most severe economic downturn since the Great Depression. Under George W. Bush's administration, the housing market collapsed, banks failed, and millions of Americans lost their homes. The crisis was caused, in large part, by the deregulation of the financial industry that began under Reagan and continued under Bush. The housing bubble, fueled by risky mortgage lending and speculative investment, eventually burst, leading to widespread economic devastation.

As economist Joseph Stiglitz argues in *The Price of Inequality*: "The 2008 financial crisis was the inevitable result of an economic system that had been designed to serve the interests of the few, at the expense of the many" (Stiglitz, 2012). The crisis demonstrated, once again, the inherent instability of capitalism, as the very institutions that were supposed to provide stability—banks and financial markets—had become the engines of destruction. The collapse of Lehman Brothers, the bailout of financial institutions, and the subsequent recession revealed the deep flaws in the capitalist system and its inability to provide for the needs of the people.

Trump and the Illusion of Economic Prosperity

Donald Trump's presidency was marked by a return to right-wing economic policies, including massive tax cuts for the wealthy and deregulation. Trump's economic policies, like those of Reagan and Bush before him, promised to create jobs and stimulate growth. However, these policies were primarily designed to benefit the wealthy and corporations, with little regard for the working class. While the stock market saw significant gains during Trump's presidency, wages stagnated, and inequality continued to rise.

Trump's economy, like Reagan's and Bush's, relied on the notion that wealth would "trickle down" to the rest of society. This idea, which has been thoroughly debunked, assumes that by benefiting the rich and corporations, wealth will eventually "trickle down" to the working class. However, in practice, this has never happened. Instead, the rich have become richer, and the poor have become poorer. The stock market may have soared, but the vast majority of Americans saw little improvement in their standard of living.

Biden's presidency, in contrast, has been focused on addressing the economic inequality exacerbated by Trump's policies. Biden's American Rescue Plan, which included direct stimulus payments to Americans and expanded unemployment benefits, was a direct response to the economic devastation caused by the COVID-19 pandemic and the policies of the previous administration. Biden's policies, unlike those of his predecessors, seek to provide a safety net for working-class Americans and reduce the wealth gap that has been widening for decades.

Capitalism's Decline: From Crisis to Collapse

The structure of modern capitalism has entered an era where contradictions are becoming ever more apparent. This stage of capitalism—late-stage capitalism—is marked by the increasing centralization of wealth in the hands of a few while vast swaths of the population are left to struggle with stagnant wages, unemployment, and the growing alienation that often accompanies precarious labor. Capitalism, once a system of growth and expansion, has reached a saturation point in many of the world's economies. As corporations continue to consolidate and monopolize entire sectors, the question remains: can capitalism survive when the people it depends on no longer have the resources to sustain it?

The 2008 financial crisis, triggered by a housing bubble built on predatory lending, was a flashpoint that exposed the fragility of the global capitalist system. The bailout of banks and financial institutions at the expense of ordinary people led to widespread disenchantment and distrust in the system. In the aftermath of the crisis, while the rich rebounded quickly through government bailouts and stock market growth, the working class saw little relief. Unemployment remained high, wages stagnated, and the wealth gap widened. The inability of the capitalist system to rectify these imbalances highlighted a fundamental flaw: the system thrives on inequality and the extraction of value from labor, but when that labor becomes less valuable due to automation, outsourcing, and economic instability, the system begins to break down.

As economist Robert Reich argues in *Saving Capitalism: For the Many, Not the Few*, the neoliberal economic policies of the last few decades have created a system that rewards the rich and punishes the poor. "The top 1 percent now owns more wealth than the bottom 90 percent combined, and that wealth continues to grow while wages for the working class stagnate" (Reich, 2015). This concentration of wealth in the hands of a few has led to what is now referred to as the "K-shaped recovery," where those at the top continue to thrive while the rest of society sees little to no progress.

Fascism as Capitalism's Last Resort

The collapse of capitalism, or at least the inability of capitalism to fulfill the promises of equality, opportunity, and fairness, has often led to the rise of authoritarian and fascist movements. History has shown us that when capitalism reaches a point where it can no longer maintain the illusion of upward mobility for the working class, those who benefit from the system turn to more drastic measures to maintain control. The rise of fascism in Europe during the 1920s and 1930s, particularly in Nazi Germany, was, in many ways, a response to the failures of capitalism and the subsequent collapse of the political and economic order.

In Germany, after the First World War, the Treaty of Versailles imposed crippling reparations on the German people, leading to hyperinflation, widespread unemployment, and the erosion of the middle class. The Weimar Republic, established after the war, struggled to provide basic social welfare, and its failure to address the needs of the people created a fertile ground for far-right ideologies to take root. Adolph Hitler's Nazi Party capitalized on this discontent, offering scapegoats for the economic collapse—namely, Jews, communists, and other marginalized groups—and promising a return to national greatness. This move was less about a true ideological commitment to fascism and more about a desperate attempt to preserve the capitalist order in the face of a collapsing social and economic system.

In *The Origins of Totalitarianism*, political theorist Hannah Arendt discusses how fascism operates as a form of "capitalism in crisis," wherein the ruling elite uses authoritarian means to restore order and protect their wealth. She writes, "The rise of fascism is capitalism's final response to the social revolution of the working class. It is a form of capitalist reaction in the face of the collapse of liberal democracies" (Arendt, 1951). The state, in this context, becomes an instrument for the protection of economic elites, using nationalism, militarization, and suppression of dissent to maintain the system.

The rise of fascism in Europe is not an isolated phenomenon. Similar dynamics have played out throughout history, particularly during periods of economic instability. When capitalism begins to fail, and when democratic institutions are no longer able to provide solutions to the economic crisis, it creates a vacuum that can be filled by authoritarian figures or movements. These movements offer simple answers to complex problems, using scapegoating, fear, and nationalism as tools to unite a disillusioned populace under a banner of totalitarianism.

The Parallel Between Fascist Germany and Modern America

The United States today finds itself in a situation strikingly similar to that of Weimar Germany in the early 20th century. The country is facing severe economic inequality, social division, and political instability, while the ruling elite continues to concentrate wealth and power. The rhetoric of populist movements, particularly the rise of figures like Donald Trump, taps into the frustrations of the working class, offering solutions that emphasize nationalism, militarization, and the scapegoating of marginalized groups. Like Hitler, Trump's rise is inextricably linked to a system that has failed to deliver on its promises of opportunity and prosperity for the masses.

In his book *The Road to Serfdom*, economist Friedrich Hayek argues that fascism is the inevitable result of government intervention in the economy and the breakdown of capitalist institutions. While Hayek's argument is often used by proponents of neoliberalism to justify minimal government intervention, it is equally useful in understanding the connection between capitalist crisis and authoritarianism. Hayek writes, "The greater the state's intervention in the economy, the greater the risk of authoritarian rule. When capitalism fails, it paves the way for fascism" (Hayek, 1944).

The events of January 6, 2021, when a mob of Trump supporters stormed the U.S. Capitol in an attempt to overturn the results of a democratic election, serve as a stark reminder of how quickly democracy can be undermined when economic and social instability converge with political disillusionment. The insurgency was not just a protest against an election result; it was a manifestation of the broader frustration and fear many Americans feel in the face of a collapsing system. The actions of the Capitol rioters were fueled not just by political ideology but by the economic disempowerment of large swaths of the population, who feel alienated from a system that no longer serves them.

The Dangers of Rising Authoritarianism in America

America's current trajectory mirrors many of the conditions that made fascism attractive to the German people in the 1930s. The ruling class, in the face of mounting dissatisfaction, seeks to maintain its power through authoritarian means. This is evident in the increasing militarization of the police, the erosion of democratic norms, and the rise of anti-democratic rhetoric in the political mainstream. As the political scientist Noam Chomsky argues in *Requiem for the American*

Dream, "We are seeing a sharp turn toward authoritarianism in the United States. The combination of economic inequality, political polarization, and a lack of trust in democratic institutions sets the stage for authoritarian movements to take root" (Chomsky, 2017).

The American response to this looming crisis, however, is not necessarily one of despair. Rather, it presents an opportunity to reimagine and reform the economic system itself. The failings of capitalism, both in the U.S. and globally, have become increasingly undeniable. The concentration of wealth in the hands of a few, the decline of the working class, and the increasing fragility of democratic institutions point to the necessity of an economic system that is more equitable and sustainable.

Building a Post-Capitalist Future: The Need for Reformation

If capitalism, in its current form, is unable to provide for the needs of the people, it is time to explore alternatives. The rise of social movements around the world, from Occupy Wall Street to the resurgence of democratic socialism, suggests that there is growing momentum for a rethinking of economic systems. A post-capitalist society, built on principles of fairness, equality, and sustainability, offers a potential way forward.

Economists like Thomas Piketty, in *Capital in the Twenty-First Century*, argue that the solution lies in progressive taxation, wealth redistribution, and a reevaluation of the fundamental role of capital in our society. Piketty suggests that the concentration of wealth in the hands of the few is not just a result of market forces but of policy choices that benefit the rich. By implementing policies that prioritize the welfare of the many over the profits of the few, it is possible to create a more equitable society.

One potential model for a post-capitalist society is democratic socialism, which combines democratic governance with a more equitable distribution of wealth and resources. Social democratic countries in Europe, such as Sweden and Denmark, have demonstrated that it is possible to have a robust economy while ensuring that the needs of the people are met through universal healthcare, free education, and strong social safety nets. The idea is not to destroy capitalism entirely but to reform it into something that serves everyone, not just the elite.

The Path Forward

The decline of capitalism and the rise of authoritarian movements are not inevitable. Rather, they are the product of a system that prioritizes profit over people, power over equality, and greed over social welfare. The solution to these crises is not to embrace fascism, but to embrace change—a radical rethinking of how economies and societies function.

By recognizing that capitalism, as it exists today, is failing to meet the needs of the people, we can begin to chart a new path forward. This path requires bold thinking, collective action, and a willingness to challenge the status quo. The future is not predetermined, but it is shaped by the choices we make today. As history has shown, we have the power to build a better world—a world in which everyone can thrive, not just the wealthy few.

The lesson from history is clear: when capitalism fails, when it becomes a tool for the enrichment of a small elite, the dangers of fascism and authoritarianism grow. The choice is ours: continue down the path of inequality and authoritarianism, or work together to build a future based on justice, equality, and the well-being of all.

Chapter 6: The Intertwining of Capitalism and Modern Society: A Portrait of a Broken System

Modern society as we know it today is intricately woven into the fabric of capitalism. It is impossible to understand the issues facing our world without first examining how the economic systems we live under shape everything from our daily lives to our broader societal values. Capitalism, an economic model based on private ownership, competition, and profit maximization, has created a global economic system that profoundly affects nearly every aspect of our social, political, and cultural lives.

Capitalism, at its core, creates a world where the accumulation of wealth is the primary goal, often at the expense of human dignity, sustainability, and equality. This economic system, though highly successful in generating material wealth and technological innovation, also fosters vast disparities in wealth and power, with its benefits overwhelmingly skewed toward the rich. What is often overlooked, however, are the myriad consequences that stem from this system's inherent contradictions: the unequal distribution of resources, the concentration of wealth in the hands of a few, environmental degradation, and the erosion of social and community bonds. These systemic issues, exacerbated by the relentless pursuit of profit, have created an unstable, unsustainable, and, in many ways, broken world.

As we explore the intertwining of capitalism and modern society, we will see how the very framework that promises prosperity has led to an array of social, political, and environmental crises. The effects of these intertwined forces are visible in every corner of our world today, from the anxiety-inducing cycles of economic boom and bust to the deepening inequality that leaves millions struggling, to the environmental degradation threatening our planet's future. What we are witnessing is the systemic failure of capitalism, a failure that is becoming increasingly difficult to ignore. It is no longer a question of whether capitalism works, but rather whether it is sustainable in the long term, both socially and ecologically.

The Core Issue: Capitalism and Social Inequality

One of the most fundamental contradictions at the heart of capitalism is its ability to concentrate wealth and power in the hands of a few while leaving the vast majority of people with little to no control over their economic lives. In a capitalist society, wealth is accumulated through private ownership of the means of production and the exploitation of labor. Those who own capital—be it land, factories, or intellectual property—are able to extract wealth from workers, who, in turn, are paid wages that often fail to reflect the value of the labor they provide. This results in the growing inequality that defines capitalist economies.

Economist Thomas Piketty, in his groundbreaking book *Capital in the Twenty-First Century*, argues that capitalist economies are inherently prone to increasing inequality. Piketty's research reveals that when the rate of return on capital exceeds the rate of economic growth, wealth becomes increasingly concentrated in the hands of the already wealthy. The problem, Piketty argues, is that as wealth accumulates in a few hands, the rest of society becomes poorer, and economic opportunities for the majority shrink (Piketty, 2013). This dynamic is not just a feature of modern capitalism—it is a structural aspect of the system that has been in place for centuries. Capitalism, by design, fosters inequality because it rewards ownership over labor.

The economic policies of the past few decades in many capitalist societies have made this inequality even more pronounced. In the United States, for example, tax cuts for the rich, deregulation of industries, and the outsourcing of manufacturing jobs have all contributed to the wealth gap. According to the Economic Policy Institute, the top 1% of income earners in the U.S. saw their incomes grow by 157% from 1979 to 2018, while the bottom 90% saw their income grow by only 22% during the same period (Mishel et al., 2020). The result is a system where the rich continue to get richer, while the poor and middle class struggle to maintain their standard of living.

Moreover, this inequality is not only economic—it is social and political as well. As wealth becomes increasingly concentrated at the top, so too does power. The rich can use their economic power to influence political decisions, ensuring that the policies enacted favor their interests. A study by Gilens and Page (2014) found that the preferences of the wealthiest Americans are much more likely to influence government policy than those of the general public. This creates a system of "economic democracy" in which only those with money have a voice, leaving the majority of people without the ability to affect the policies that govern their lives.

This inequality is not just a matter of financial disparity—it has far-reaching consequences for social stability and cohesion. As the rich accumulate wealth, they not only gain economic power but also political power, further entrenching their position at the top of society. This creates a feedback loop where those at the top of the economic ladder influence policies to further their own interests, often to the detriment of the broader population.

For instance, the 2017 Tax Cuts and Jobs Act, passed under the Trump administration, exemplified how tax cuts for the wealthy exacerbate inequality. According to the Congressional Budget Office (CBO), the top 1% of income earners received about 40% of the benefits from the tax cuts, while the bottom 80% received just 19% of the benefits (CBO, 2018). These policies were justified as a means of stimulating economic growth, yet the reality is that they disproportionately benefited the wealthy, further exacerbating the wealth gap.

Capitalism does not merely create wealth—it creates winners and losers, and its structure reinforces this divide. The accumulation of wealth by the top 1% leads to a systematic breakdown in social mobility, as opportunities for advancement become increasingly scarce for the lower and middle classes. What was once a belief in the "American Dream"—the idea that anyone can succeed through hard work—is increasingly becoming a myth in a capitalist society where privilege, inherited wealth, and access to resources determine success, rather than merit alone.

Capitalism and the Dismantling of Social Welfare Systems

Another critical aspect of modern capitalism is the dismantling of social safety nets and public welfare systems. While the promise of capitalism is that market competition will drive innovation and improve services for everyone, the reality is that the privatization of essential public goods has left many without access to basic needs. This is especially true in sectors like healthcare, education, and housing, where the profit motive often takes precedence over human well-being.

The United States offers a stark example of the failure of capitalism to provide for the basic needs of its citizens. In healthcare, for instance, the privatization of the system has led to high costs, limited access, and uneven quality of care. According to the Commonwealth Fund, the U.S. spends more on healthcare than any other country, yet its healthcare outcomes are far below those of other industrialized nations. As of 2020, nearly 30 million Americans were uninsured, and millions more were underinsured, unable to afford the high costs of care (Collins et al., 2020). The result is a healthcare system that benefits the wealthy and leaves the rest of society to fend for itself.

Similarly, the cost of higher education in the U.S. has skyrocketed over the past few decades. As public universities have increasingly relied on tuition revenue to fund their operations, the cost of education has risen to levels that are unaffordable for many. According to the Federal Reserve, student loan debt in the U.S. reached $1.7 trillion in 2021, affecting more than 45 million borrowers (Federal Reserve, 2021). This massive debt burden prevents young people from achieving financial independence, homeownership, and other markers of economic success. As with healthcare, the privatization of education has created a system where access to opportunity is determined not by merit but by one's ability to pay.

The privatization of housing has had similar effects. In many urban areas, the rise of real estate investment trusts (REITs) and corporate landlords has driven up rental prices, making it increasingly difficult for working-class families to find affordable housing. According to the National Low Income Housing Coalition, there is a shortage of 7 million affordable rental homes in the U.S., with the gap growing every year (NLIHC, 2021). This crisis has led to widespread homelessness, particularly in major cities like San Francisco and New York, where rent prices have become unaffordable for the majority of residents.

These trends reflect a broader shift away from the concept of public goods and social safety nets toward a privatized system where access to basic services depends on one's ability to pay. This shift has been facilitated by neoliberal economic policies that prioritize market competition over collective well-being. As a result, the most vulnerable members of society—those who need healthcare, education, and housing the most—are often left without access to the resources they need to live healthy, stable lives.

The profit-driven motives of privatization also create significant inefficiencies. Public services, when adequately funded and designed to serve the common good, can operate at a much lower cost and more equitably than for-profit alternatives. However, the privatization model incentivizes cutting corners and creating services that serve only those who can afford them. This, in turn, exacerbates inequality and undermines the social contract that binds a society together.

Capitalism and the Environmental Crisis

Perhaps one of the most urgent challenges facing modern society is the environmental crisis, which has been exacerbated by the logic of capitalism. The capitalist imperative for constant growth and the extraction of resources from the Earth has led to widespread environmental degradation, including deforestation, pollution, and climate change. The relentless pursuit of profit has made short-term economic gain a priority, often at the expense of the long-term health of the planet.

Climate change is perhaps the most obvious manifestation of the environmental crisis. According to the Intergovernmental Panel on Climate Change (IPCC), the world has already warmed by 1.1°C above pre-industrial levels, and global temperatures are projected to rise by another 1.5°C to 2°C by 2050 (IPCC, 2021).

This warming is already having devastating effects on ecosystems and human societies, including rising sea levels, extreme weather events, and widespread displacement.

Capitalism, as it currently functions, has contributed to this crisis in several ways. First, the system relies on the exploitation of natural resources, often in unsustainable ways. Fossil fuel extraction, deforestation, and industrial agriculture all contribute to the degradation of the environment. Second, the drive for profit encourages corporations to externalize environmental costs, meaning that the negative effects of industrial activity are borne by society, not the corporations themselves. For example, the oil and gas industries have been responsible for significant pollution and carbon emissions, yet these costs are not reflected in the price of fossil fuels, allowing companies to continue polluting the environment without bearing the full consequences of their actions.

The capitalist focus on constant growth also exacerbates the environmental crisis. Economic growth, in the capitalist sense, is measured by an increase in production and consumption. However, this growth is unsustainable in a finite world, where resources are limited. The capitalist need for perpetual expansion runs counter to the reality that the Earth's resources are finite. As a result, the pursuit of endless growth leads to environmental depletion, contributing to climate change, loss of biodiversity, and pollution.

Capitalism and Mental Health

The relentless pressures of capitalism take a psychological toll on individuals. The constant drive for productivity and success in an increasingly competitive world has led to a mental health crisis. Studies have shown that the pursuit of material wealth and status can lead to feelings of inadequacy, loneliness, and depression. The psychological stress of living in a society where success is measured by financial achievement has been linked to increased rates of anxiety, depression, and substance abuse.

According to the American Psychological Association (APA, 2017), economic stressors are strongly associated with mental health problems. Financial instability, job insecurity, and the pressure to perform at work create an environment in which people feel anxious, exhausted, and overwhelmed. The constant drive to "keep up" with others, driven by consumerism and materialism, leaves people feeling disconnected from their true selves and trapped in a cycle of unfulfilling labor. The overwhelming sense of inadequacy and anxiety that pervades modern life is a direct result of the pressures imposed by capitalism.

The Need for Change

Capitalism, while driving technological innovation and economic growth, has also generated deep systemic inequalities, environmental destruction, and widespread psychological distress. The very structures that were designed to create prosperity have, in reality, left many people behind and created a world marked by fear, uncertainty, and instability. This system is no longer sustainable. The growing wealth divide, the dismantling of social safety nets, the environmental crisis, and the mental health epidemic are all symptoms of a deeper, systemic failure. Capitalism, in its current form, is incompatible with a just, sustainable society.

The path forward requires a radical rethinking of our economic systems. We need to prioritize human well-being, environmental sustainability, and social justice over the pursuit of profit. Only by addressing the root causes of inequality, environmental degradation, and psychological distress can we hope to build a future that benefits everyone, not just the few at the top. This will require bold reforms, collective action, and a willingness to challenge the status quo. The alternative—continuing down the path of exploitation and destruction—will only lead to more suffering and instability.

The road to a better future is not easy, but it is possible. The time to act is now. If we are to build a world that prioritizes people over profits, cooperation over competition, and sustainability overgrowth, we must begin the work of dismantling the capitalist system that has brought us to this point. Only then can we create a future that is just, equitable, and sustainable for all.

Chapter 7: The Course of Action: Rebuilding a Just and Sustainable System

The urgency of addressing the entrenched failures of capitalism cannot be overstated. As the foundations of modern society crack beneath the weight of a system that prioritizes profit over people and exploitation over well-being, we find ourselves at a crossroads. The inequalities, environmental degradation, and systemic flaws embedded in capitalism require not only critique but active and deliberate efforts toward reform or even dismantling. The nature of these systemic issues calls for a multi-faceted approach—ranging from revolutionary change to gradual reform. These efforts must aim not only at economic fairness but also at transforming the social, environmental, and political structures that sustain capitalism's dominance.

This chapter explores the broad range of potential courses of action that can lead us away from the capitalist framework and toward a more just and sustainable world. A complete restructuring, though formidable, is possible—and necessary. From the critical analysis of existing governmental structures to the proposal of alternatives that would be better equipped to address modern crises, this chapter will outline a variety of systems and evaluate them through evidence, history, and practical considerations. By acknowledging that no system is without flaws, we can engage in a comprehensive search for solutions—some more radical than others, but all aimed at achieving a more balanced, equitable society.

Understanding Capitalism's Flaws

Capitalism has been hailed for its ability to generate wealth and foster innovation, but this success comes at a massive cost. The system's core principle is the generation of profit, which often means the prioritization of capital accumulation over human rights, environmental sustainability, and social equity. The structural inequalities that have emerged in capitalist economies are a direct result of the capitalist emphasis on profit maximization.

Inequality and Concentration of Wealth

The capitalist system has led to a profound concentration of wealth in the hands of a small elite. In 2021, Oxfam reported that the wealthiest 1% of the world's population controlled 38% of global wealth, while the bottom half owned just 2%. This wealth inequality is not a byproduct of capitalism but its direct consequence. Capitalism inherently drives the accumulation of wealth at the top, with those who own the means of production reaping the largest rewards, while workers see little to no increase in their wages despite contributing to economic growth.

This wealth inequality is not only financially crippling but socially destabilizing. The resulting inequality prevents equal access to education, healthcare, and opportunities for advancement, creating a vicious cycle that traps people in poverty. Furthermore, it has led to a rise in social unrest and division, as economic disparity fuels resentment and alienation.

Exploitation of Labor

At the heart of capitalism is the exploitation of labor. Under capitalism, workers—who constitute the majority—are paid far less than the value of their output. According to Karl

Marx's theory of surplus value, workers create value through their labor, but only a fraction of that value is returned to them in wages. The rest is taken by the owners of capital, making labor a key source of capitalist profit.

The global workforce is increasingly facing precarious labor conditions, particularly in the gig economy, where workers are treated as independent contractors rather than employees. Studies from organizations such as the National Employment Law Project (2020) have shown that gig workers face wage theft, a lack of benefits, and exploitation from platforms like Uber, Amazon, and other gig economy giants. These workers are vulnerable to constant economic insecurity and, despite their efforts, remain trapped in cycles of poverty.

Moreover, the neoliberal push for deregulation in labor markets has exacerbated these conditions. The reduction in union power and labor protections has left workers with little recourse to demand better wages or working conditions. The gig economy and the rise of temp work have made stable, secure employment a thing of the past for many people.

Environmental Destruction and Capitalism's Growth Imperative

Capitalism's relentless pursuit of profit has also led to widespread environmental destruction. From deforestation to pollution, capitalism's insatiable demand for resources has stretched the planet's ecosystems beyond their capacity to recover. Economic growth, the primary objective of capitalist economies, is inherently incompatible with sustainability. The capitalist emphasis on infinite growth—particularly in sectors like fossil fuels, agriculture, and manufacturing—leads to the overexploitation of natural resources and a disregard for the long-term consequences.

The Intergovernmental Panel on Climate Change (IPCC, 2019) warns that global warming needs to be limited to 1.5°C to avoid catastrophic environmental damage. However, under capitalism, economic policies often prioritize short-term profits over the long-term well-being of the planet. Major corporations, particularly in the fossil fuel industry, have long been complicit in delaying action on climate change. As recently as 2020, ExxonMobil was found to have misled the public about the dangers of climate change, despite internal research indicating that fossil fuels were a major contributor to global warming.

The environmental consequences of this unchecked growth are already being felt, from rising sea levels to extreme weather events and widespread biodiversity loss. The capitalist economic model, which emphasizes profit over ecological responsibility, is a central driver of the environmental crisis.

Exploring Alternative Systems: What Works Better Than Capitalism?

Capitalism is not the only economic system that has been tried—and it certainly isn't the only one that can work. History offers us many examples of alternative systems, each with its own strengths and weaknesses. The following section explores several of these systems, evaluating them in terms of how well they address the systemic issues inherent in capitalism, including inequality, labor exploitation, and environmental degradation.

Revolution: Dismantling the System

The most radical course of action is a revolutionary transformation—a complete dismantling of the capitalist system. Revolutions have historically been viewed as a way to overthrow the entrenched power structures that perpetuate inequality and oppression. Though the specter of revolution is often associated with violence and chaos, it is important to examine revolutionary movements that have aimed to bring about meaningful change in more peaceful, democratic ways.

The Russian Revolution of 1917, for instance, was initially a movement aimed at redistributing power to the working class. While the Bolshevik regime eventually devolved into authoritarianism under Stalin, the revolution itself was a response to a deeply unjust system of feudalism and capitalism. Similarly, the

Cuban Revolution sought to eliminate the domination of foreign capital in Cuban society and redistribute wealth more equitably. Despite its flaws, the Cuban model has succeeded in offering free healthcare, education, and social welfare to its citizens—accomplishments that capitalism has failed to replicate.

The key challenge for any revolution is ensuring that the process does not result in the consolidation of power in the hands of a new elite, but rather in the redistribution of power to the masses. A revolutionary model would need to center on the collective ownership of resources, democratic governance, and workers' control over the means of production.

Social Democracy: A Middle Path

Social democracy is a more gradual approach to transforming society, one that accepts the existence of capitalism but calls for policies to curb its most damaging effects. Social democracy advocates for strong labor protections, universal healthcare, free education, progressive taxation, and wealth redistribution through social welfare programs. Countries like Sweden, Denmark, and Finland have implemented social democratic policies that promote greater equality while retaining a capitalist economic framework.

The success of social democracy in these countries can be attributed to the ability to balance market forces with strong social programs. By investing in education, healthcare, and infrastructure, social democracies have managed to create more equitable societies, reduce poverty, and improve quality of life for all citizens. These nations have also maintained high standards of living, though critics argue that they are still vulnerable to capitalist pressures such as the privatization of public goods and rising inequality.

While social democracy does not fundamentally challenge capitalism, it offers a pragmatic alternative that can address the worst excesses of the system, particularly when it comes to inequality and access to essential services.

Democratic Socialism: Worker Control

Democratic socialism is an alternative system that seeks to eliminate the capitalist ownership of the means of production, replacing it with democratic control by the workers. In this system, workers would collectively own and manage industries, ensuring that profits are distributed equitably and that economic decisions are made with the welfare of all in mind, rather than the interests of a few wealthy individuals.

Worker cooperatives, such as the Mondragón Corporation in Spain, have shown that this model can function on a large scale. Mondragón, a federation of worker-owned businesses, has been in operation for over 60 years and employs tens of thousands of workers. This cooperative structure ensures that decision-making power is decentralized and that profits are reinvested into the community rather than being extracted by external shareholders.

Democratic socialism allows for the redistribution of wealth and the elimination of private ownership of key industries, which would help to solve the problem of wealth concentration. While challenges remain—such as scaling the model to larger economies and ensuring equitable access to resources—democratic socialism offers a compelling alternative to capitalist exploitation.

Eco-Socialism: A Green Future

Eco-socialism combines the goals of environmental sustainability with socialist principles. It advocates for a post-capitalist society that addresses both the ecological crisis and the economic inequality caused by capitalism. Eco-socialists argue that a sustainable future requires an economy based on renewable energy, public transportation, sustainable agriculture, and the protection of biodiversity. This economic transformation requires not only a shift away from fossil fuels but also a radical restructuring of how we produce and consume goods.

Eco-socialism offers a solution to the environmental crisis by ensuring that growth does not come at the expense of the planet's health. By shifting to a steady-state economy focused on human welfare rather than profit maximization, eco-socialism seeks to balance human needs with ecological preservation. The Green New Deal, proposed in the U.S., is an example of eco-socialist thinking in practice—focusing on the creation of green jobs, renewable energy, and social justice.

A Transition to a Just Society

No matter which course of action we pursue—whether revolution, reform, democratic socialism, or eco-socialism—the goal remains the same: the creation of a just society where economic systems no longer exploit people or the planet. As we move forward, it is crucial to integrate these systemic alternatives into the conversations about modern society's issues, from economic inequality to climate change. Each of these systems, while flawed, presents pathways to a future where resources are shared, power is democratized, and ecological sustainability is prioritized.

Chapter 8: Reflections on Modernity

In the distant quiet, far from the digital frenzy, the noise of daily life, and the buzz of notifications, there comes an unsettling realization: we are living in an age where we've lost sight of what it truly means to exist. In a world dominated by the relentless pursuit of progress and achievement, we find ourselves drowning in a sea of demands. And no matter how hard we swim, we never seem to reach land. Every day, we are told we need more. More success, more possessions, more achievements, more validation. Yet, every step we take toward these hollow goals only leads us further away from the one thing we need most: ourselves.

We are in the midst of a constant struggle, not for survival, but for recognition. The digital age promises connection, yet it only amplifies our loneliness. The speed of life, the constant rush to do more, to be more, leaves us with nothing but exhaustion and a lingering sense of emptiness. The modern world has placed its value on what we do—what we produce, what we consume, what we contribute. But the more we do, the further we drift from the very essence of our being. We've traded our souls for a fleeting sense of accomplishment.

The Facade of Progress

The relentless obsession with progress has become the foundation of our existence. It isn't just about career advancement or wealth accumulation—it's about the endless race. The idea that forward motion is the only path to meaning. From the moment we open our eyes, we are thrust into the demands of a world that rewards achievement over humanity. We wake up and the first question is, "What have I done today?" Not, "How do I feel?" or "What do I need?" It's a world where our worth is determined by how much we can produce and how fast we can do it.

This isn't just a personal struggle—it's a societal one. We live in a world where rest is a luxury, not a necessity. Where reflection is seen as indulgence, not a vital component of mental and emotional health. We've been conditioned to think that slowing down is a weakness. A moment spent not working, not achieving, is viewed as wasted time. It's a vicious cycle—one that eats away at our well-being and steals our ability to enjoy the present. We're not given the space to simply *be*. We're taught that our value lies in how much we can do, how much we can contribute to the machine.

And what happens when we can't keep up? When the demands of modern life become too much? We collapse. We burn out. The system we've so diligently tried to satisfy shows us no mercy. It moves on, as cold and indifferent as ever, leaving us behind to pick up the shattered pieces of ourselves.

The Silent Cost of Overachievement

We've been sold the lie that more is always better. More money, more success, more recognition. But every step we take in the pursuit of more takes us further from what we truly need. More doesn't fill the emptiness. It only highlights it. This unrelenting push for progress, for achievements, for accumulating wealth, leaves us exhausted, hollow, and disconnected from what really matters. The more we gain, the more we lose.

In the pursuit of more, we sacrifice the things that make us human. Relationships. Connection. Peace. The ability to sit in silence and reflect without the constant buzz of to-do lists and deadlines. We're told that happiness lies in the things we can acquire. But what happens when we have it all—and it still doesn't feel like enough?

We've become a society of empty vessels, filled only with the relentless pursuit of a goal that doesn't even exist. We chase after the illusion of success, thinking that once we reach it, we'll be fulfilled. But the closer we get, the more we realize that success isn't a destination—it's a trap. A trap that keeps us running until we're too tired to care, and too lost to know who we even are anymore.

It's like a scene out of *American Psycho* (2000)—the more Patrick Bateman achieves, the more he loses himself. The manic pursuit of wealth, status, and recognition becomes a self-destructive force. His life is a constant exercise in acquiring, achieving, and consuming, but it leads him nowhere. It's a perfect metaphor for the capitalist system: an endless chase for something that can never truly satisfy. We strive for more, but the more we get, the emptier we become.

The Power of Slowing Down

But what if we could stop? What if we could throw off the chains of productivity and learn to exist in the moment? What if we could step off the treadmill and just breathe? In a world that demands constant motion, it's not enough to simply rest. We must *reclaim* stillness. We must give ourselves permission to stop, to reflect, to be present without guilt. The world won't stop spinning because we choose to rest, but in that stillness, we might just find the clarity and peace we've been searching for.

In *The Secret Life of Walter Mitty* (2013), the protagonist breaks free from the monotony of his life and embraces adventure and stillness. The moments of reflection in his journey are as important as the action. There's a power in being present, in stepping away from the noise and allowing ourselves to reconnect with our true selves. This is the path to healing, to regaining our humanity, and to finding meaning that goes beyond the shallow promises of success.

We are not machines. We are human beings. And in our pursuit of progress, we've forgotten that. We've been trained to ignore the whispers of our soul, to drown out the quiet calls for rest and reflection with the constant clamor of modern life. But it's in those moments of quiet, of stillness, that we can begin to hear the things that truly matter. The things that don't come with a price tag.

Capitalism's True Cost

What we've failed to understand is that the system, at its core, doesn't care about us. It doesn't care about our mental health, our happiness, or our fulfillment. It cares about what we can produce. It cares about how much we can give to the machine. Our worth is measured in output, not in being. And as long as we continue to chase after that illusion of progress, we will never escape the grip of a system that values productivity over humanity.

We've been conditioned to believe that we are only valuable when we are doing something. When we're producing, consuming, achieving. But this belief comes at a cost. It robs us of the ability to simply be. It steals our joy, our peace, and our ability to connect with others on a meaningful level. We become mere cogs in a machine, defined by our roles rather than our humanity.

The price of capitalism is steep—it's not just economic, it's existential. It's the loss of our sense of self. The sacrifice of our well-being. And ultimately, it's the forfeiture of the things that make life truly worth living.

The End of the Race

And then the question becomes—what happens when we stop? What happens when we reject the endless pursuit of more? What happens when we decide that we've had enough of the rat race, enough of the chasing, enough of the noise?

Is it possible to opt out? To refuse to play the game and still find meaning in life?

And if we do, what are we left with?

Maybe that's the scariest part—what if we choose to stop, and we find there's nothing left for us? What if the world we've been racing toward is nothing but an empty shell?

In *Requiem for a Dream* (2000), the characters chase their dreams, only to find that their desires destroy them. The pursuit of happiness, of success, of the ideal life—it all leads to despair. The system promises everything but delivers nothing. And in the end, they are left with nothing but their own brokenness.

But what if that's exactly what we need? What if stopping, letting go, and finding peace in stillness is the key to unlocking the truth of who we are?

Is it worth the risk?

Or are we too afraid to find out?

What happens when we stop pretending?

What happens when we stop chasing the illusion?

And finally—what if, after all this time, we find that the answer was never in the race?

What if it was always on pause?

Are we brave enough to stop and face that? Or will we keep running?

And what if the machine doesn't let us go?

And after all of this. After all of these ideas to fix the system and modern society.

Just stop. Just be.

Sincerely,